CW01067040

Croner's Guide to COSHH

R. M. Pybus

Croner Publications Limited
Croner House
London Road
Kingston upon Thames
Surrey KT2 6SR
Telephone: 081–547 3333

First published 1991
Second Edition 1993

Published by
Croner Publications Ltd,
Croner House,
London Road,
Kingston upon Thames,
Surrey KT2 6SR
Telephone 081–547 3333

While every care has been taken in the writing and editing of this book, readers should be aware that only Acts of Parliament and Statutory Instruments have the force of law, and that only the courts can authoritatively interpret the law.

British Library Cataloguing in Publication Data
Pybus, R. M.
Croner's guide to COSHH.
I. Title
363.17

ISBN 1–85524–237–0

Printed by Whitstable Litho, Whitstable, Kent.

Contents

We would like to acknowledge the assistance of Paul Reeve, BSc, MSc, CChem MRSC, MIOSH, Head of Safety and Environment at the Engineering Employer's Federation, London SW1, and Croner's Health and Safety Department for their assistance in the compilation of this book.

Chapter 1
Introduction

What is COSHH?

COSHH must by now be one of the better known occupational safety and health acronyms. It stands for the Control of Substances Hazardous to Health Regulations 1988. It was enacted through the broad framework of the Health and Safety at Work, etc Act 1974 (the HSW Act). COSHH is an extension of the duties of employers and employees described in ss. 2 and 7 of the 1974 Act respectively, but applying specifically to damage to health through exposure to hazardous substances.

Supporting the COSHH Regulations there are, to date, six Approved Codes of Practice (ACOPs). The first is a General Approved Code of Practice which enlarges on the broad duties described in the Regulations themselves. The second is a Carcinogens Approved Code of Practice which applies to a limited number of specific substances and processes. The others are even more specific and deal with fumigation operations, vinyl chloride monomer, potteries and the use of non-agricultural pesticides respectively. There are more ACOPs in the pipeline.

In addition, there is an increasing amount of practical guidance from the Health and Safety Executive (HSE) which, together with local authorities, enforces the Regulations.

Why is COSHH important?

Although there has always been a general requirement under the HSW Act for employers to ensure, so far as is reasonably practicable, the health and safety at work of employees, and for employees to co-operate with the employer in fulfilling this duty, the means of doing so have generally been left to the discretion of the employer. Exceptions were those substances or processes which were the subject of specific legislation, such as The Control of Asbestos at Work Regulations 1987 and the Radioactive Substances Act 1960. COSHH places more detailed duties on the employer and employee, but particularly the employer, to prevent, or adequately control, exposure of employees to substances which are hazardous to health, through a process of assessment and control.

To comply with COSHH an employer must be able to demonstrate that hazards have been identified and the risks formally assessed, that specific control measures have been put in place and that these measures are effective. The most practical way of doing this is by writing down the assessment and by recording how exposure to hazardous substances is being controlled. Such an assessment would certainly be requested by an inspector (either the Health and Safety Inspector or the local Environmental Health Officer depending on the type of premises). So it is worthwhile having a simple, formal method for COSHH assessments to make the job easy and to show to the enforcing authorities (and, if things do go wrong, the courts) that all "reasonably practicable" steps to comply with the Regulations have been taken.

What is the scope of COSHH?

COSHH applies to virtually all substances which present a health hazard to employees at work, including special hazards such as biological agents. Some parts of the Regulations apply also to persons other than employees who may be affected by those substances. The only exceptions to the Regulations are those substances which are the subject of specific or more detailed legislation, such as lead and asbestos, or hazards such as ionising radiation. Some hazardous substances are subject to more detailed provisions under Approved Codes of Practice issued under the COSHH Regulations — examples are vinyl chloride and carcinogenic substances.

There is no limit on quantity to the application of COSHH.

The overriding principle is that if a substance is a hazard to health, its use must be assessed.

The Regulations apply as much to the self-employed as they do to other employers. As far as COSHH is concerned, the self-employed person is regarded as both the employer and the employee.

Basically, COSHH is concerned with substances which are either toxic, harmful, corrosive or irritant. It is not concerned with substances which do not have these properties, even though they may be hazardous in other ways — flammable, for example.

What is a "substance hazardous to health"?

A "substance hazardous to health" is just that – any substance, in whatever form, which presents a hazard to health. This is a patently obvious and broad statement, but it is essentially what the Regulations mean. Admittedly, they go to rather greater lengths in defining "substances hazardous to health", but in the final analysis if a substance can damage health, it falls within the scope of the Regulations. So corrosive acids, toxic gases, wood dust and solvent-based typists' correction fluid, for example, all fall within the scope of COSHH.

Further details about how to identify hazardous substances are given in Chapter 2.

How do the Regulations affect employers?

Employers are required at least to control the exposure of their employees to substances hazardous to health, with the aim of preventing exposure, or reducing it to an acceptable minimum. They are expected to do this not primarily by providing employees with personal protective equipment (PPE), but by "at source" methods, such as modifying a process so that the hazardous substance is contained, or using exhaust ventilation. Protective equipment or clothing is regarded as a last resort.

For some substances maximum exposure limits (MELs) are prescribed, usually expressed in terms of parts per million (ppm) or milligrams per cubic metre (mg m^{-3}) in the atmosphere. For these substances employers are expected to ensure that employees are exposed to the minimum practicable level, but in any case not above the MEL. Where personal protection is required it must be suitable and of an approved type (either by the HSE or the British Standards Institution). Employees must understand the risks involved from hazardous substances either used or generated in the workplace and the precautions required to prevent or minimise exposure.

The other requirements on employers, discussed in later chapters, are to check that control measures for preventing exposure are actually working — from checks on hardware, to exposure monitoring, to medical monitoring of employees (in certain cases) — and to keep records of the checks which have been made.

Are there special cases?

Earlier we examined briefly the scope of COSHH and identified that certain hazardous substances were subject to their own individual regulations (eg asbestos and lead). A few substances are banned from certain uses (almost all are carcinogens) and these are listed in schedule 2 of the COSHH Regulations. There are just three other situations where the Regulations do not apply. The first is where the risk to health relates to a substance being taken in the course of medical treatment. The second is in mines, where the Mines and Quarries Act 1954 applies. The third is to the master and crew of seagoing ships.

Showing compliance with the Regulations

Compliance has to be demonstrated. This means keeping records of risk assessments for the substances hazardous to health which are being used or generated, and of the means by which the risk is eliminated or reduced to an acceptable level. The results of any atmospheric or medical monitoring which has been carried out should be recorded to demonstrate that the control measures are working, together with the results of maintenance checks on ventilation equipment designed to reduce exposure to substances hazardous to health.

Making records to demonstrate compliance with the Regulations is explored in more detail later in the book.

The Management of Health and Safety at Work Regulations 1992 have introduced a requirement for employers to carry out a general risk assessment, and the COSHH assessment is an integral part of this overall approach. Where a COSHH assessment has been carried out, it does not have to be repeated to satisfy the requirements of the 'Management Regulations', but it should be easily cross-referenced with the general assessment.

Where to start

It is helpful to use a step by step approach to the subject, so the following logical process has been chosen:

(a) identify the hazardous substances
(b) identify properties and hazards
(c) identify the work activities (in which substances hazardous to health are used or generated)
(d) assess the risks
(e) inform employees
(f) reduce risk by simple change
(g) control the residual risks
(h) check the effectiveness of control measures
(i) health surveillance
(j) records
(k) auditing the procedures which have been put in place.

Each step of the process will be dealt with by an individual chapter in this book; at the end of the process readers should have a clear idea of how to go about applying COSHH to their own workplace activities.

Chapter 2
Identify the hazardous substances

- ▸ **Identify the hazardous substances**
- Identify properties and hazards
- Identify the work activities
- Assess the risks
- Inform employees
- Reduction of risk by simple change
- Control the residual risks
- Check the effectiveness of control measures
- Health surveillance
- Records
- Auditing the procedures which have been put in place

To understand the process by which the risk of damage to health by exposure to hazardous substances may be assessed we need to be clear about the difference between hazard and risk.

Hazard is the potential of something to do harm. As an example of hazard, consider the bleach in a household bottle. This is a hazard because it is capable (it has the potential) of damaging the skin. Whilst the bleach remains unused in the bottle, however, it cannot do any damage, so it does not present a risk. It is only when the bleach is used that it presents a *risk* because then there is a probability of exposure to the substance. Whether that probability is high or low will depend on how the bleach is used and in what quantity.

So, the *risk* of damage from any substance is dependent on a number of factors:

(a) its *hazardous properties* (what damage – injury – it can cause to the body through its chemical properties)

(b) its *physical form*
(c) the *quantity* used
(d) the *activities* (how it is used).

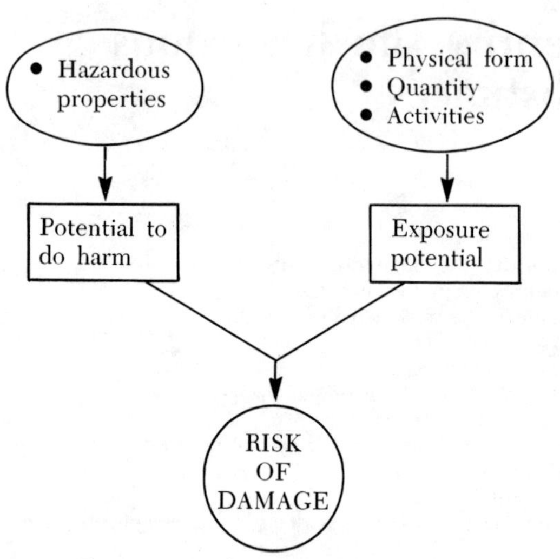

Figure 1: Simple risk assessment model

The model in Figure 1 is a simple representation of how the factors combine to create risk. It will be used later when, in Chapter 3, we explore how to identify the properties and hazards of substances (the "potential to do harm" aspect of the model), in Chapter 4 when we explore activities (the "exposure potential" of the model) and in Chapter 5 when we look at ways of calculating the risk of damage.

Now we will take a look at each of the above four factors briefly in turn.

Hazardous properties

The properties of a substance which enable it to damage the body in some way are the health hazards of that substance. The principal hazardous properties are:

(a) irritant
(b) corrosive
(c) toxic.

Substances which are *irritant* usually have a short term effect which is reversible when exposure to the substance is removed. Ammonia gas is an irritant in low concentrations, for example.

Substances which are *corrosive* can irreversibly damage the body chemically. An example is skin burns from exposure to a strong acid. Such damage is not reversible and the affected area of skin will only be repaired by regeneration of the damaged skin tissue, providing that the damage is not too severe.

Substances which are *toxic* affect the chemical processes within the body when they gain entry by some route (skin absorption, ingestion or inhalation). The degree of damage depends on the consequences of the interference with the body's natural chemical processes. Some toxic substances have a relatively small effect – simple petroleum solvents for example – and some, such as cyanide, have a profound effect in very small quantities. Some toxic substances such as ammonia have short-term effects and others have long-term effects – benzene is a notable example.

Some substances display more than one property. Benzene has a short-term narcotic effect and a long-term health effect. Short-term exposure to benzene causes drowsiness and sickness, symptoms which will gradually disappear when exposure is removed; but repeated, significant exposure over long periods of time can cause blood cancer.

Finally, some substances act as "sensitisers". Following exposure to a sensitising substance, certain individuals suffer adverse reaction to subsequent exposures at levels (often extremely low levels) which previously resulted in no adverse effect.

The COSHH Regulations define a "substance hazardous to health" as any substance, or mixture of substances, which is:

(a) listed in Part 1A of the HSE "approved list" as dangerous for supply within the meaning of the Classification, Packaging and Labelling of Dangerous Substances Regulations 1984 and for which the general indication of the nature of the risk is specified as very toxic, toxic, harmful, corrosive or irritant

(b) a substance for which a maximum exposure limit is specified in schedule 1 of the COSHH Regulations or for which the Health and Safety Commission has approved an occupational exposure standard

(c) a micro-organism which creates a hazard to health

(d) dust of any kind when present at a substantial concentration in air

(e) a substance, not being a substance mentioned in (a) – (d) above, which creates a hazard to health which is comparable with the hazards created by substances mentioned in (a) – (d).

In later chapters we will come back to the "approved list" and "Scheduled" list of substances. These name specific substances and describe particular hazardous properties: (e) above tells us that even if a substance is not listed, it is still a "substance hazardous to health" if it has similar hazardous properties to any of the listed substances. Unless a substance is essentially harmless, therefore, it falls within the scope of the Regulations.

Physical form

The physical form of a substance determines how it may enter the body to do damage. Substances which enter the body most easily are those which are in a form which enables them to be inhaled — gases, vapour, aerosols and fine dusts are prime examples. Some substances are naturally gaseous, some liquid, some solid.

Next, we shall examine each physical form in turn to see how it can exert a damaging effect on the body.

SOLIDS
- contact with the skin
- absorption through the skin
- inhalation as dust

LIQUIDS
- contact with the skin
- absorption through the skin
- inhalation as an aerosol

GASES
- contact with the skin
- absorption through the skin
- inhalation

All three forms can impact on the body by:
(a) skin contact
(b) skin absorption
(c) inhalation

Solids

It is easy to see how solid substances can affect the skin by simple contact and how, if they are in a very finely divided form, they can be inhaled. Solid substances do not usually transport through the skin, but if they are dissolved in a solvent which itself passes easily through the skin, they can be transported as well.

Liquid

Again, skin contact and inhalation through finely divided droplets (aerosol) are obvious risks. Skin absorption is very dependent on the nature of the substance. The skin has some natural resistance to liquid penetration, but certain liquids, especially those which do not mix readily with water, enter the skin quite easily. Some liquids can dissolve and remove the skin's natural oils and fats, making it dry and more liable to cracking. In this state it is less resistant to penetration by other substances.

Gases

Corrosive gases (such as hydrogen chloride) can do straightforward damage to the skin. Gases can also penetrate the skin, although this is dependent on their properties. However, both these effects are relatively insignificant compared with inhalation, which is the principal route of entry into the body for a gas. Some asphyxiant gases, such as nitrogen or carbon dioxide, can damage the body by excluding the oxygen the body needs for respiration. Although this hazardous property is not covered by COSHH, it should be considered whenever people are working in confined spaces.

Quantity

Put simply, the more of a substance one works with, the greater the potential for exposure.

Activities

How a substance is used has a significant effect on the potential for exposure to it. Take two simple examples.

(a) If hardwood is planed, the shavings present no hazard to health; if it is sanded with a power operated sanding machine, finely divided hardwood dust will be generated which is a hazard to health through inhalation.

(b) If an organic cleaning solvent is used at room temperature, there will be some potential for exposure by inhalation because of the solvent vapour. If the process requires the solvent to be heated, however, more vapour is given off and the potential for exposure is therefore greater.

These two examples show that activities may not only increase the potential for exposure to a hazardous substance, but may also *create* a hazard (such as the generation of wood dust in (a)) which was not previously present.

Hazards outside the scope of COSHH

The COSHH Regulations are only concerned with the control of substances which are hazardous to health by their contact with, or entry into, the body. The scope of this book is confined, therefore, to the consideration of the risk to health presented by these substances and to their containment. It should not be overlooked, however, that substances have other properties which are hazardous to people in other ways. Flammability is an obvious example — careless use of flammable liquids can cause substantial injury and damage. The total risk management of a business needs to take all the hazards into consideration.

Summary

In this chapter we have explored the difference between *hazard* and *risk*, the factors which make up the risk, and the components of a simple model which illustrate the way in which these factors combine to create the risk. The next chapter deals with gathering information about the physical and hazardous properties of substances hazardous to health.

Chapter 3
Identify properties and hazards

- Identify the hazardous substances
- ► **Identify properties and hazards**
- Identify the work activities
- Assess the risks
- Inform employees
- Reduction of risk by simple change
- Control the residual risks
- Check the effectiveness of control measures
- Health surveillance
- Records
- Auditing the procedures which have been put in place

Carrying out a risk assessment requires a knowledge of the properties of the substances being used. This chapter deals with the identification of the physical form and the hazardous properties of substances. Look back to Figure 1 on page 8 to see where they fit into the risk assessment model.

What physical properties do we need to know?

In the last chapter we explored briefly how the physical form of a substance determines how it may enter the body to do damage (the *route* of exposure). It is necessary to know enough about the physical properties of each substance being used or produced to understand what that route of exposure is likely to be.

The main physical properties of substances, when considering exposure potential, are:

(a) the melting point
(b) the boiling point and
(c) the normal vapour pressure.

In the case of solids, the particle size, and sometimes the crystalline form, can be important. The melting point can also be significant: moving from one physical form to the other greatly affects the mobility of the substance and can, as a result, affect the ease of its containment.

A more important property is the boiling point. Above this temperature the substance is naturally a gas rather than a liquid. The lower the boiling point, the more volatile the substance. The more volatile the substance, the higher its concentration in the air at a given temperature and therefore the greater the potential for exposure through inhalation.

Heating a liquid will increase its concentration as a gas in the air. The higher the temperature of the liquid, the closer it approaches its boiling point and the more rapidly it vaporises. As before, this results in an increasing risk of exposure.

For solids, a significant property is particle size. Some solids form dust easily and others are sold in a finely divided form because that is how they are used — fillers and reinforcers for rubbers and plastics are examples. When dusts reach a certain small size they become "respirable", that is they are able to penetrate deep into the lung cavities. Dusts of particle size this small are often difficult to see, which can reduce the caution which might otherwise be taken. Some solids of respirable particle size are very hazardous because of their capability of penetrating into the lungs.

Finding information about physical properties

Information about the physical properties of commercially available substances is relatively easy to acquire. The simplest way to the information is through the supplier, who should be able to supply a product safety data sheet on request. This should provide details about the physical, chemical and hazardous properties of the substance. (A typical product data sheet is illustrated on pages 17–19).

HAZARD DATA SHEET MERCK

Product Acetonitrile
CAS No 75–05–08

BDH Product Codes 10386–14044–15251–15266–15285–29220

– – – – –

– – – – –

HAZARD IDENTIFICATION

FLAMMABLE TOXIC

TRANSPORT INFORMATION

Hazard Class 3.2 **UN No** 1648 Pkg Group II

COMPOSITION Organic solvent

REGULATORY INFORMATION

Symbols F T Phrases R11–23/24/25
S16–27–44

PHYSICAL AND CHEMICAL PROPERTIES

Description Colourless volatile liquid, ether-like odour

M Pt (deg C) −41 **B Pt (deg C)** 80 **Specific Gravity** 0.78

Solubility in water Miscible in all proportions

Vapour pressure 100 **mmHg at** 27 deg C
Vapour density 1.42 **(air=1)**

FIRE AND EXPLOSION HAZARD Highly flammable

May evolve toxic fumes in fire

Flash point (deg C) 2
Explosive limits (%): lower 4, **upper** 16
Auto-ignition temperature (deg C) 524

FIREFIGHTING MEASURES Foam, dry powder, carbon dioxide or vaporising liquids

HEALTH HAZARD Toxic by inhalation, ingestion and skin contact, causing fatigue, nausea, diarrhoea and abdominal pain. In severe cases there may be delirium, convulsions, paralysis and coma.

TOXICOLOGICAL INFORMATION

Toxicity data	LD50	2730	mg/kg oral, rat
	LC50	13	mg/l inh rat

Carcinogenicity No evidence of carcinogenic properties
Mutagenicity/Teratogenicity Evidence of teratogenic effects

FIRST AID MEASURES

Eyes Irrigate thoroughly with water for at least 10 minutes. OBTAIN MEDICAL ATTENTION.

Lungs Remove from exposure, rest and keep warm. In severe cases, or if exposure has been great, OBTAIN MEDICAL ATTENTION.

Skin Drench the skin thoroughly with water. Remove contaminated clothing and wash before re-use. Unless contact has been slight, OBTAIN MEDICAL ATTENTION.

Mouth Wash out mouth thoroughly with water and give plenty of water to drink. OBTAIN MEDICAL ATTENTION.

STABILITY AND REACTIVITY

Stability Stable

Reaction with water Will react with hot water and steam giving toxic and flammable vapours.

Other known hazards

Can react vigorously with oxidising materials. Forms potentially explosive mixtures with *N*-fluoro compounds. Produces violent exothermic reaction with sulphuric acid and with sulphur trioxide.

Avoid contact with: **Water** (no) **Acids** (no) **Bases** (no) **Oxidisers** (yes) **Combustibles** (no)

ACCIDENTAL RELEASE MEASURES

Precautions Shut off all sources of ignition
Inform others to keep at a safe distance
Wear appropriate protective clothing

If local regulations permit, mop up with plenty of water and run to waste, diluting greatly with running water. Otherwise absorb on an inert absorbent, transfer to container and arrange removal by disposal company. Ventilate area to dispel residual vapour.

For large spillages liquids should be contained with sand or earth and both liquids and solids transferred to salvage containers. Any residues should be treated as for small spillages.
If material has entered surface drains it may be necessary to inform local authorities, including fire services if flammable.

DISPOSAL

Dispose of through local authorities if appropriate facilities are available, otherwise pass to a chemical disposal company.

EXPOSURE CONTROLS AND PERSONAL PROTECTION - as appropriate to quantity handled

UK Exposure limits OES, mg/m^3 (Long-term 8hr TWA) 70

Respirator	Self-contained breathing apparatus
Ventilation	Fume-cupboard, flameproof
Gloves	Nitrile
Eye protection	Goggles or face shield
Other measures	Plastic apron, sleeves, boots — if handling large quantities

ECOLOGICAL DATA

Not implemented

STORAGE AND HANDLNG

Special requirements
In accordance with the Highly Flammable Liquids and Liquefied Petroleum Gases Regulations 1972. In accordance with HSE guidance note CS17.

Date 14/06/90 **Sheet No** 01641

Reproduced by permission of Merck Ltd.

If more extensive information about physical properties is required (for example, the vapour pressure of a substance at a particular temperature), the supplier may not be able to help, and this may mean resorting to scientific reference texts. Alternatively, a good, all-round chemical and physical data reference book, such as the International Technical Information Institute *Toxic and Hazardous Industrial Chemicals Safety Manual* can be invaluable.

Also, trade and employers' associations are a potential source of information.

What information about hazards is needed?

In Chapter 2 we looked at the basic hazardous properties of substances, and classed them broadly as irritant, corrosive and toxic. To gain a sufficient understanding of the hazards of a substance, three factors need to be known:

(a) the action the substance has on the body (the basic hazardous properties)
(b) how severe that action is
(c) whether there are any established and accepted limits on exposure to the substance.

The basic hazardous properties should be indicated on the label of the container of the substance. The Classification, Packaging and Labelling of Dangerous Substances Regulations 1984 schedules a comprehensive list of substances for which standard hazard and safety phrases are required. Typical hazard warning labels are shown in Figure 2 (although not in colour). Diamond shaped labels are United Nations symbols and square labels are EC symbols. The label may also identify by what means the substance is hazardous (eg "causes burns" or "toxic by inhalation") and what precautions to take in handling it. However, even if there is not much detail on the label, more hazard information should be available from the supplier of the substance.

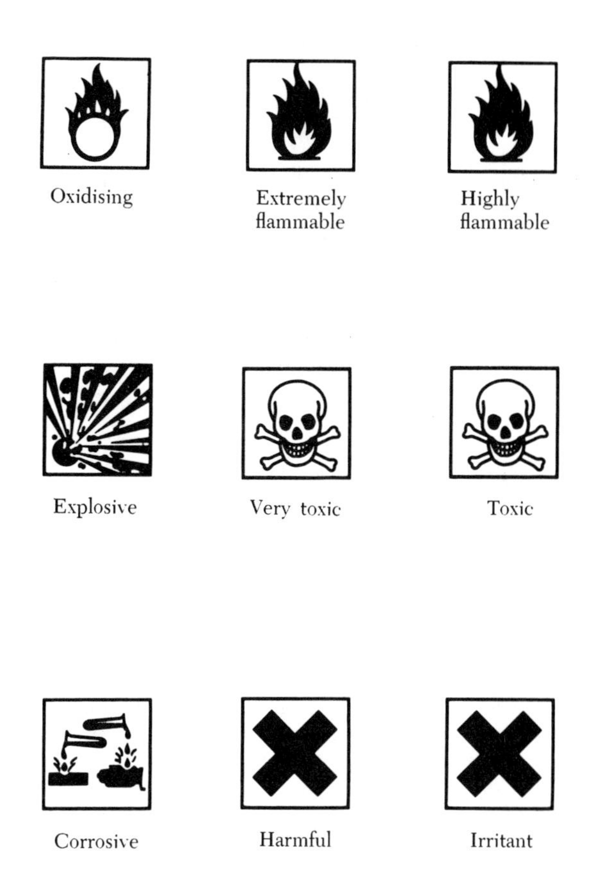

Figure 2 Hazard warning labels

These are black on an orange background. Note that similar symbols vary slightly in their meaning.

Duty of supplier

The supplier has a duty under s. 6 of the Health and Safety at Work, etc Act 1974 to provide "... adequate information about the results of any relevant tests which have been carried out [on the substance] ... and about any conditions necessary to ensure that it will be safe and without risks to health when properly used".

So, if the supplier of a substance is asked for health and safety information then, within reason, that supplier is duty bound to provide it. Sometimes the physical and hazard data is contained on a single product data sheet. Often, the product data sheet will include recommendations on the safe handling of the substance and sometimes gives information on what action to take if it is spilled, or the emergency action to take if a person is exposed. It may also give guidance on disposal of the substance.

Finding more detailed toxicological information

It is important to know the seriousness of the impact that the substance hazardous to health has on the body. This information is sometimes given in a general way on the product data sheet. For example, the words "highly corrosive" or "highly toxic" will indicate that the corrosive or toxic effect is serious, but that may not be enough to help someone to decide accurately the extent of the hazard. More precise hazard information (mainly on toxic substances) is available for many commercially available substances, but this may not be on the product data sheet. This extra information may come in two forms – occupational exposure standards and animal testing data.

Occupational Exposure Standards

A good place to look is the Health and Safety Executive's Guidance Note EH40, which gives Occupational Exposure Standards for a wide range of substances and Maximum Exposure Limits (MEL) for a limited number. The Occupational Exposure Standards (OES) indicate the upper limit of airborne exposure (in terms of ppm or mg m^{-3} in the air), both for long-term (eight hour working day) and short-term (over a ten minute period) exposure. By and large, substances with a low MEL or OES are more hazardous than those with high values. Don't forget, though, that hazardous properties are only one factor in determining the actual risk of damage to health, and that MELs and OESs only refer to airborne exposure.

Fortunately, if a common commercial substance is being used, it is very likely that it is included in the Guidance Note EH40 list of Occupational Exposure Standards. The supplier's product data sheet should be checked for the proper name of the substance (as opposed to its brand name) before looking it up in EH40.

Listed in the back of EH40 are titles of over 50 Guidance Notes on specific substances, processes and situations where exposure to substances hazardous to health can occur, including advice on control measures.

Animal testing data

If a substance is not amongst those listed in EH40, and the supplier's health and safety data sheet does not give a recommended occupational exposure standard, the only other information on its toxicity is likely to be from animal testing data. This is much less helpful information because it requires expert interpretation, based on professional judgement which must allow for a margin of error.

Other information sources

There are many reference texts, some of which are listed at the end of this chapter, on the hazardous properties of substances. In addition, there is an "Authorised and Approved List" of substances with a summary of their hazardous properties and associated safety precautions, published by the Health and Safety Commission as a guide to packaging and labelling hazardous substances. This list can be used as a check on the adequacy of the information of the label of any container of hazardous substance from a supplier.

It is always worth checking with a trade association to see what information it can provide on the hazardous properties of the substances being handled. Information can also be obtained from certain computer databases — the Sigma Aldrich database is a good example.

Summary

To summarise, information on the hazardous properties of substances can be found:

(a) on the substance container label
(b) from the supplier's health and safety data sheet
(c) from the Health and Safety Commission's "Authorised and Approved List"
(d) from the Health and Safety Executive Guidance Note EH40
(e) from trade associations
and (although probably in a less accessible form) from:
(f) chemical data reference texts
(g) computer databases of the hazardous properties of substances.

Grouping hazards by type

Grouping substances with very similar physical and hazardous properties can help simplify the risk assessment process. For example, if a company was using a range of carbon blacks in a rubber vulcanising process, it would probably be able to take them as a single substance for the purpose of risk assessment.

Substance interaction hazards

When handling more than one substance there may be the possibility of substances interacting to form new, and possibly more toxic, substances. An extreme example of this is the interaction, at normal temperature and pressure, between two very simple substances, formaldehyde and hydrogen chloride, to form bis(chloromethyl)ether (BCME). Whilst the two parent substances are themselves toxic, the product of their reaction is *extremely* toxic, with an occupational exposure standard 2000 times smaller than either of the other two substances.

Chemical intermediates and products

However, many users will be concerned simply with the use of single substances in workplace activities where there is no substance interaction to form new and different substances and, therefore, new hazards. On the other hand, some companies need chemical reactions to produce chemical products. In this case it is necessary to assess the hazards of the substances which are reacting and of the product being made. The hazards of any reaction intermediates will also need to be assessed if there is a risk of exposure to them. The same goes for any by-products of the reaction if they present a hazard to health.

Summary

In this chapter, we have examined the part that the physical form of substances and their hazardous properties have to play in the risk assessment process. We have looked at the types of physical and hazardous properties about which information is needed and where it may be found.

We have also identified the importance of not overlooking the hazards that can be presented by substance interaction and by the reaction intermediates and by-products of chemical processes.

Knowledge about substances clears only the first hurdle, however; COSHH requires an assessment of health risk arising from the *use* of substances. So, the next stage of our guide will look at *activities*.

References

International Technical Information Institute, The *Toxic and Hazardous Industrial Chemicals Safety Manual.*

Kellard B *Hazardous Substances: Carcinogens Guide*, 2nd edition, Croner Publications Ltd, 1993, ISBN 1 85524 2273.

Sax I and Lewis R J *Dangerous Properties of Industrial Materials*, 8th edition, Van Nostrand Reinhold, New York, 1992, ISBN 0 442 01132 6.
Handbook of Toxic and Hazardous Chemicals, Noyes Publications, ISBN 0 8155 0841 7.
Substances Hazardous to Health, Croner Publications Ltd, 1993, ISBN 1 85524 197 8.

Chapter 4
Identify the work activities

- Identify the hazardous substances
- Identify properties and hazards
- ► **Identify the work activities**
- Assess the risks
- Inform employees
- Reduction of risk by simple change
- Control the residual risks
- Check the effectiveness of control measures
- Health surveillance
- Records
- Auditing the procedures which have been put in place

In all businesses there are many activities. The only ones of interest as far as COSHH is concerned, however, are those in which substances hazardous to health are used or generated.

Substances and activities

To assess all the operational risks associated with substances hazardous to health, the substances must be matched with activities. This can be approached in different ways but the simplest effective method is obviously to be preferred.

There are two basic options:

(a) listing substances hazardous to health against individual activities or
(b) listing activities against individual substances.

The choice will be influenced by the relative number of substances hazardous to health and the activities in which they are used. Unless the assessment involves a very limited number of substances hazardous to health the preferred method will probably be that of listing substances against individual activities. There are two main reasons for adopting this approach.

(a) The risk of exposure to a harmful substance depends not just on the physical properties of the substance but on the way it is used. So, irrespective of the substances, each activity must be assessed because it contributes to risk.
(b) Processes themselves can generate substances hazardous to health, which may be overlooked where assessments are based on substances rather than activities.

Activity

These two statements lead us to a crucially important point: COSHH is about the *control* of substances hazardous to health, *not just the assessment* of hazards from substances. To be done properly, the emphasis must be placed on the *activity*. Where there are many different activities which use or generate substances hazardous to health, they should be broken down into manageable parts (for example by area or workplace). Then each one should be taken in turn, systematically.

For each area or workplace, every activity where exposure may occur should be written down — even the apparently simple ones. As a simple example take a paint shop where products are spray painted; this is a single process comprising a number of different activities. In this case we would probably list the following activities:

(a) decanting the paint into the spraying equipment
(b) decanting paint thinners into the spraying equipment
(c) paint spraying and
(d) cleaning out the paint spraying equipment with thinners.

There may, of course, be other activities to add to the list. The substances hazardous to health associated with each of these activities would be the paint itself (usually a complex mixture of solvents, pigments and other agents) and paint thinners (for example, cellulose thinners — a mixture of solvents).

In this way it is possible to generate a comprehensive list of activities for each workplace, with a list of the substances hazardous to health associated with each of those activities.

Using "standard assessments"

Activities, and their associated substances hazardous to health, which are common may be covered by a single assessment (a "standard" or "generic" assessment). This avoids repetition of similar assessments. Additionally, where an activity is using a range of substances with similar properties a single assessment (covering all the substances for that activity) may be all that is required, providing that the assessment covers the "worst case" (in terms of all the factors in the risk assessment model), so that it will be adequate for all the other, similar activities.

An example of a standard assessment would be the handling of photocopier chemicals in offices. Creating a standard assessment in this case should be fairly easy, since the quantities, hazardous properties, types of substance and handling methods would be very similar.

Summary

This short chapter has examined briefly the significance of activities in the risk assessment model, which either use substances hazardous to health or generate them. It has explored the options of substance-based and activity-based assessments, and makes a case (in most circumstances) for the latter. It has offered a way of simplifying the assessment workload by using "standard" assessments, where possible.

The next chapter looks at how to assess the risk of damage to health from a knowledge of the hazardous properties of substances, and of the factors that make up the exposure potential.

Chapter 5
Assess the risks

- Identify the hazardous substances
- Identify properties and hazards
- Identify the work activities
- ► **Assess the risks**
- Inform employees
- Reduction of risk by simple change
- Control the residual risks
- Check the effectiveness of control measures
- Health surveillance
- Records
- Auditing the procedures which have been put in place

Up to now the COSHH process has been straightforward, even though it may have required some effort to collect information about the physical properties and hazards of substances and to examine in detail workplace activities, in order to identify those in which substances hazardous to health are used or generated.

Usually, assessing the risk of exposure to substances hazardous to health from each of those activities is not so straightforward. It is necessary to recall the aim — to identify those substances where there may be exposure of staff (or indeed anyone else) to hazardous substances used or generated, at levels which may damage their health. Where there is a risk of this occurring, action must be taken to eliminate exposure, or at least reduce it to acceptable levels, which should be below the occupational exposure limits.

This chapter deals with assessment of the risk of damage to health using a knowledge of the properties of the hazardous substances and the activities in which they are used.

As discussed in the previous chapter, there are two ways

of approaching the combination of hazardous substances and activities. One way is to examine all the activities associated with each substance. The other is to examine the substances associated with each activity. The latter approach ("activity-based" assessments) is, as we have seen, usually the more practical, and it will be the approach taken in this guide.

What are the factors that make the risk? Going back to the simple risk assessment model (Figure 1), the principal factors which determine the risk of exposure are:

(a) the quantity being used
(b) the physical form of the substance under the conditions of use
(c) the containment capability of the activity and
(d) the damage potential of the substance (how toxic or corrosive it is).

The first three factors determine how much of the substance people are likely to be exposed to, and the last determines how serious the consequences of the exposure are.

It is necessary to put all four factors together in a way which tells us whether the activity we are studying is safe to operate as it is, or whether better control (such as ventilation) or protection is needed, or whether the hazard to health from the substance is so great that special containment is necessary.

An assessment of how the four factors combine may be made subjectively or it can be calculated. Because conclusions based on a subjective approach are difficult to justify (and demonstrate to an inspector), it is an advantage to use a quantitative (calculated) approach. Within each of the four principal factors there is a wide variation in properties which can contribute to the risk of damage to health. Take quantity, for example: handling a large quantity of a substance hazardous to health presents a much greater risk than a small quantity under similar conditions of handling. Similarly, handling a fine dust presents more of an inhalation risk than handling a dense solid, and a low containment process presents a greater risk of exposure than a high containment process.

A straightforward method of taking these wide variations into account is to divide each of the four factors into a number of clearly defined component parts, each with an assigned hazard rating. For every activity being assessed, the hazard ratings for each factor can be multiplied to give a quantitative figure which is an indication of the overall risk of damage to health from that activity and its associated substance(s) hazardous to health.

It is not intended that the approach should give a precise measurement of the risk of damage, but it does provide an *objective*, rather than subjective, appraisal of risk, based on a consideration of the contribution made to that risk by the four principal factors.

So, take each of the four factors in turn and apply the principle just described using, for ease of calculation, a factor of 10 to separate the "hazard ratings" of the component parts of each factor.

Physical form

Different physical forms present different hazards. For simplicity, the variation of hazard with physical form can be expressed as in Figure 3. Note that each hazard description is assigned a numerical "hazard rating" which relates to the physical characteristics.

Physical characteristic	Hazard description	Hazard rating
Dense solids Non-volatile liquids	Low hazard	1
Coarse dusts Volatile liquids	Medium hazard	10
Gases Highly volatile liquids Aerosols Fine dusts	High hazard	100

Figure 3 Physical characteristics

It is important to identify the physical form of the substance under the conditions of use. For example, if a substance

Figures 3–12 are adapted from grids in *COSHH in Laboratories* published by the Royal Society of Chemistry, London.

(especially a liquid) is heated, its vapour pressure will be increased and its hazard rating will rise accordingly.

Quantity

Activities may range from the use of less than a few grams of a substance (use of a small quantity of typewriter correction fluid) to kilogram quantities or much more. If we take the range of quantity from less than ten grams to over one kilogram, it can be divided into three distinct component parts:

(a) up to 10g
(b) 10g–1kg
(c) over 1kg.

For a given activity, using a few grams of a hazardous substance will represent much less of an exposure risk than using one kilogram. As with "Physical characteristic", the variation of exposure risk with quantity may be expressed as a factor of 10 in each case:

Quantity	Hazard rating
up to 10g	1
10–1kg	10
over 1kg	100

Figure 4 Quantity/hazard rating

This then gives a "hazard rating" based on the quantity of substance used.

Containment characteristic

Some activities are inherently better at containing hazardous substances than others. The variation in containment capability and the associated exposure hazard rating can be expressed in the following way (Figure 5).

Containment characteristic	**Containment description**	**Hazard rating**
Essentially closed system, where the likelihood of any significant release is very small.	High containment	1
Partially open system where, either by design or by failure of containment known to be inherent in the activity, there is likely to be a limited release of hazardous substance.	Medium containment	10
Essentially open system or high known incidence of containment failure leading to significant release of hazardous substance.	Low containment	100

Figure 5 Containment characteristic

This time we have identified a "hazard rating" based on the containment capability of the activity.

Exposure potential

Before considering what is probably the single most important factor — the *damage potential* of the substance hazardous to health — let us combine the hazard ratings of the three exposure potential factors using the table in Figure 6. From this table the overall "exposure potential" may be calculated.

Hazard rating / **Exposure potential factor**	**1**	**10**	**100**
Quantity	Up to 10g	10g–1kg	Greater than 1kg
Physical form	Low hazard	Medium hazard	High hazard
Containment capability	High	Medium	Low

Figure 6 Hazard rating/exposure potential factor

The overall exposure potential may be calculated as:
"quantity" hazard rating × "physical form" hazard rating × "containment" hazard rating.

If the overall exposure potential is less than, or equal to 100 (10^2), the exposure potential is deemed to be *low*.

If the exposure potential is 1000 (10^3), the exposure potential is *medium*.

If the exposure potential is equal to or greater than 10,000 (10^4), the exposure potential is *high*.

The next stage is to categorise the damage potential of the substance used in, or generated by, the activity, from a knowledge of the hazardous properties.

Damage potential

From a knowledge of the hazardous properties of the substances (Chapter 3), their damage potential can be described in the following way (Figure 7).

Damage potential	Type of hazardous property
Very high (HH)	Potent carcinogens or toxins Respiratory sensitisers Occupational Exposure Standard (OES) of <0.1ppm (<0.5mg/m^{-3})
High (H)	Substances classified under "CPL"[1] as toxic/very toxic/corrosive Skin sensitisers OES[2] of 0.1–10ppm (0.5–50mg/m^{-3})
Medium (M)	Substances classified under "CPL" as harmful/irritant OES of 10–500ppm (50–2500mg/m^{-3})
Low (L)	Substances not meeting the "CPL" classification criteria OES of >500ppm (>2500mg/m^{-3})

[1] Classification, Packaging and Labelling of Dangerous Substances Regulations 1984 (see Chapter 3)

Figure 7 Damage potential

If it is not possible readily to categorise the damage potential of any substance being used, refer the judgement to an occupational hygienist or professional toxicologist.

Having identified, for each of the substances used in an activity, the overall exposure and damage potential, the risk of damage from the combination of the two can be expressed numerically from 1 to 3 as follows (Figure 8).

	LOW	MEDIUM	HIGH
HH	2	3	3
H	1/2	2	3
M	1	1/2	2
L	1	1	1/2

Overall exposure potential

Figure 8 Damage potential/overall exposure potential

If the risk of damage is shown as "1" the activity is probably safe to continue without any changes, although the need for personal protective equipment should be considered where accidental exposure may occur through skin contact, absorption or by inhalation.

If the risk of damage is "2", the activity requires better control of hazards to make it acceptable (for example, by ventilation), in addition to consideration of personal protective equipment as a short term solution.

Where the risk of damage is "1/2" it is necessary to decide, from the categorisation of the exposure potential factors and the damage potential, whether the weighting is towards the 1 or the 2.

If the risk of damage is "3", changes should be made to the activity as a matter of urgency to bring the hazards under control, with adequate personal protective equipment being used to protect employees in the meantime. Circumstances may require the activity to cease until adequate controls have been established.

Here are some examples applying the risk assessment process we have outlined.

Example 1

The first example is a simple one. A secretary is using typewriter corrector fluid which contains a chlorinated solvent (1,1,1-trichloroethane) — a volatile liquid with an Occupational Exposure Standard (OES) of 10ppm. It is used relatively infrequently, and in very small quantities – less than one gram at a time.

From the information we have, we can use the exposure potential table to identify the overall exposure potential.

Hazard rating / Exposure potential factor	1	10	100
Quantity	Up to 10g	10g–1kg	Greater than 1kg
Physical form	Low hazard	Medium hazard	High hazard
Containment capability	High	Medium	Low

Figure 9 Hazard rating/exposure potential factor

The quantity hazard rating is 1, the physical form (a volatile liquid) has a hazard rating of 10, and the containment capability rating is 10 because the use of the substance on the paper is limited — the majority is enclosed in the bottle.

The overall exposure potential is therefore $1 \times 10 \times 10 = 100$, which is *low*. The OES of 10ppm puts the substance as borderline between high hazard (H) and medium hazard (M). So, using the damage potential/exposure potential table in Figure 10 the risk of damage, on balance, is "1", indicating that the activity can continue unchanged, which is what one might expect from knowledge of the activity.

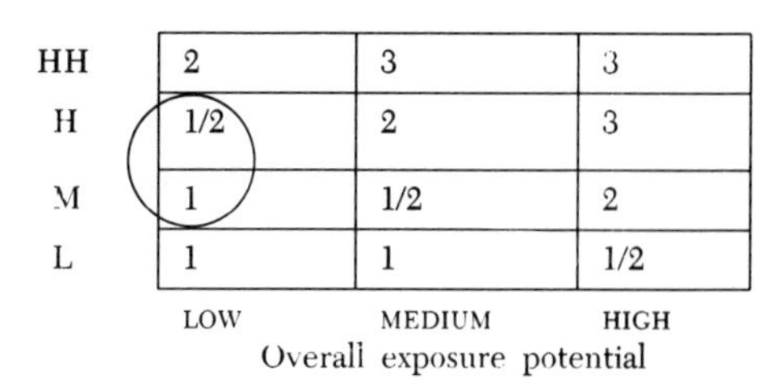

Damage potential	LOW	MEDIUM	HIGH
HH	2	3	3
H	1/2	2	3
M	1	1/2	2
L	1	1	1/2
	Overall exposure potential		

Figure 10 Damage potential/overall exposure potential

Example 2

A wood finishing operation uses a power sanding machine on hardwood furniture components. Currently the operation has no dust extraction and although the quantity of dust which gets into the atmosphere is unknown, knowledge of the scale of the operation tells the COSHH assessor that the amount of fine (respirable) dust is certainly going to be above 10 grams. Using the exposure potential table (Figure 9) the quantity hazard rating is 10, the physical form (a respirable dust) has a hazard rating of 100 and the containment capability is 100 because there is no dust extraction. The overall exposure potential is $10 \times 100 \times 100 = 10^5$, which represents *high* exposure potential.

The Maximum Exposure Limit (MEL) for hardwood dust is 5mg m^{-3}, making its damage potential category high hazard (H) – hardwood dust can be carcinogenic. Referring to the damage potential/exposure potential table (Figure 11), the risk of damage to health is serious, and immediate changes must be made to the activity to reduce the danger. The obvious action to take is the installation of extraction ventilation for the operation, and to introduce personal protective equipment (approved dust masks) for the operators until the efficiency of the extract ventilation has been established by atmospheric monitoring.

Damage potential	HH	2	3	3
	H	1/2	2	(3)
	M	1	1/2	2
	L	1	1	1/2
		LOW	MEDIUM	HIGH
			Overall exposure potential	

Figure 11 Damage potential/overall exposure potential

Example 3

A pulp bleaching operation uses chlorine gas supplied from cylinders of liquid chlorine. The operation is carried out in a large, mainly enclosed, stirred vat, with chlorine dispersed into the pulp through metal dip-pipes. Some escape of chlorine occurs through ports in the top of the vat.

About 1kg of chlorine is used during the batch bleaching operation and less than 1% (10 grams) of the chlorine escapes into the vapour space in the vat. Using the exposure potential table (Figure 6) the quantity hazard rating is 1, the physical form (a gas) has a hazard rating of 100, and the containment capability is 10 because it is a partially closed system.

The overall exposure potential is $1 \times 100 \times 10 = 10^3$, which is a *medium* exposure potential. The Occupational Exposure Standard of chlorine is 1ppm, making its damage potential category high hazard (H). From the damage potential/ exposure potential table (Figure 12) the risk of damage to health is "2", which indicates that the process should be examined to improve the exposure potential so that the level of chlorine in the atmosphere is well below 1ppm. Until this is achieved, the process operators should wear suitable respiratory equipment.

Damage potential		LOW	MEDIUM	HIGH
	HH	2	3	3
	H	1/2	(2)	3
	M	1	1/2	2
	L	1	1	1/2

Overall exposure potential

Figure 12 Damage potential/overall exposure potential

Chlorine gas has a low odour threshold and so its presence in the atmosphere is easily detected. However, some hazardous substances have odour thresholds which are greater than their Occupational Exposure Standard, so that they may be in airborne concentrations which are damaging to health without being detected. Other substances have no odour at all, so give no warning at any level.

In this example only one activity is assessed. Another activity may involve the opening up of the vats, above the pulp slurry, exposing the air space which may be heavily laden with chlorine gas. This activity, which may have a greater exposure potential, would have to be assessed separately.

Now let us go back to the paint spraying operation mentioned in Chapter 4. For the sake of argument, let us assume there are four activities associated with the operation:

(a) decanting paint into the spraying equipment
(b) decanting paint thinners into the equipment
(c) the spraying itself and
(d) cleaning the equipment with thinners.

The substances hazardous to health are the solvents which make up the paint thinners: there are three of these solvents, all of which are volatile liquids in the following proportions and with the following Occupational Exposure Standards (OESs).

Solvent	% of total thinners	OES (ppm)
A	50	100
B	40	1000
C	10	50

Figure 13 Solvent/percentage of total thinners

In our example 1kg of paint and 500g of thinners are decanted, and 100g of thinners are used to clean out the equipment; the paint composition is essentially the same as that of the thinners. We will also assume that the decanting operations are partially closed (from one "closed" vessel to another) and that the spraying and cleaning operations are essentially open, with only natural ventilation to help disperse solvent vapour and paint/solvent aerosol.

On this basis we can tabulate an assessment of the component activities (Figure 14). The results clearly indicate (as we would expect) that there is a need for careful control of the spraying operation in particular, where exposure to solvent vapour and paint in aerosol form is high.

The most common form of control would be to carry out the spraying operation in an effectively ventilated enclosure. Once this has been installed, the assessment should be carried out again, when the containment hazard rating could well reduce from 100 to 1, bringing the overall exposure potential down from 10^5 to 10^3 (medium hazard rating) for the most hazardous activity — spraying. This would reduce the risk of damage from 2 to 1/2, when a judgement would have to be made about further containment (or respiratory protection) based on atmospheric monitoring.

Decanting operations represent shorter duration exposure, but still present a significant risk of damage to health. These operations should therefore be carried out using effective ventilation. The objective of engineering controls (enclosure ventilation of local exhaust ventilation, for example) is to reduce the risk of inhalation sufficiently to avoid the need for respiratory protection. Where this can be achieved, periodic monitoring of the atmosphere will be necessary to check that the exposure levels of the solvents are well below their Occupational Exposure Standard or Maximum Exposure Limit.

Personal protective equipment in the form of solvent resistant gloves and suitable eye protection would be necessary for all the activities — including decanting — and this should be specified on the assessment form. Where atmospheric monitoring is specified, the type and frequency of monitoring should also be specified on the assessment.

Having provided effective engineering control, probably in the form of a ventilated enclosure, all the activities should be carried out in it. Sufficient detail about the engineering control should be noted on the assessment, so that it can be easily referenced to its testing and maintenance record (Chapter 10).

Activity	**Decanting paint**			**Decanting thinners**			**Spraying**			**Cleaning**		
	Solvents			Solvents			Solvents			Solvents		
Main hazardous substances	A	B	C	A	B	C	A	B	C	A	B	C
"Quantity" hazard rating	10	10	10	10	10	10	10	10	10	10	10	1
"Physical form" hazard rating	10	10	10	10	10	10	10^2	10^2	10^2	10	10	10
"Containment" hazard rating	10	10	10	10	10	10	10^2	10^2	10^2	10^2	10^2	10^2
Overall exposure potential	10^3	10^3	10^3	10^3	10^3	10^3	10^5	10^5	10^5	10^4	10^4	10^3
Damage potential	M	L	M	M	L	M	M	L	M	M	L	M
Risk of damage (risk assessment)	1/2	1	1/2	1/2	1	1/2	2	1/2	2	2	1/2	1/2

Note: 10^2= 100
10^3= 1000
10^4= 10,000, etc

Exposure potentials: 10^2 — LOW
10^3 — MEDIUM
10^4 up — HIGH

Figure 14 Activity/decanting paint/decanting thinners, etc

Medical monitoring should be made unnecessary by the introduction of engineering controls, by confirmation of the effectiveness of the control by atmospheric monitoring and by use of the personal protective equipment specified on the assessment form.

Do hazardous substances in storage need to be assessed?

If there is no risk of exposure to stored hazardous substances, then there is no need to assess: assessment is required only where the substances are being used. If the containment of a storage vessel is suspect, however, and lack of containment could give rise to exposure to a substance hazardous to health, then that must be assessed (and the containment made good).

Summary

In this chapter we have explored a process which provides a simple quantitative assessment of the risk of damage to health from the combination of the damage potential of the substances, their quantity and physical form, and the containment capability of the activity being assessed. The outcome of this process is an indication of what action may be necessary to reduce the risk of damage to health through exposure. It will always be necessary to use judgement as part of this process, especially in borderline cases (no method can cover every situation). Where there is no reasonable certainty that exposure is controlled, monitoring will need to be carried out.

Chapter 6
Inform employees

- Identify the hazardous substances
- Identify properties and hazards
- Identify the work activities
- Assess the risks
- ▶ **Inform employees**
- Reduction of risk by simple change
- Control the residual risks
- Check the effectiveness of control measures
- Health surveillance
- Records
- Auditing the procedures which have been put in place

Introduction

This chapter explores briefly the advantages of consulting with employees and the requirements that COSHH places on employers to inform, instruct and train employees (and others who may be affected) about risks to health and the measures to protect against those dangers.

Employee consultation is introduced in this chapter because employers can often help in the next stage of the reduction of risk by a process of simple change (Chapter 7). Instruction and training of employees is dealt with more fully in Chapter 8.

Information on risks to health

Not surprisingly, since COSHH is aimed at their protection, employees (and others who may be at risk) are frequently referred to in the Regulations. The employer has a duty to inform, instruct and train employees in such a way that they understand the risks to health presented by exposure to substances hazardous to health in the workplace. The employer must also ensure that employees understand the precautions which they must take to protect against that exposure.

Employees themselves have a duty to make full use of any control measures or protective equipment provided by the employer to control exposure to substances hazardous to health provided it is reasonable to do so.

It is in the long-term interest of the employer to involve employees as fully and as early as possible in the COSHH assessment process. Because employees usually have a practical understanding of the processes they are operating, they may be able to identify simple means of reducing workplace hazards. The process of involvement in finding solutions to the problems of exposure to hazardous substances will often generate the commitment to using the protective measures that are decided on the basis of the activity risk assessment.

In any event, the employer must inform employees of the hazards to which they may be exposed, what control measures will be taken to eliminate or reduce that exposure below accepted limits, and what the employees have to do to use those control measures effectively.

Information on control measures

Having made a risk assessment of each activity and given some consideration to the options for reducing the risks to acceptable levels, then employees should be consulted about control measures. Employees may already have been involved in the assessment process as part of the collection of data on the activities in which substances hazardous to health are being used. This early involvement is valuable since employees will be aware from that point on of the interest in their protection, so that later discussion of the risk assessments and the control measures could be easier.

Having explained to employees the results of the risk assessment, how it was carried out, and the conclusions, their co-operation should be sought in exploring options for changing the process, however simple, as the first stage in reducing risk. Remember that the COSHH Regulations require, so far as is reasonably practicable, that the prevention, or at least adequate control, of exposure of employees to substances hazardous to health shall be secured by means other than the provision of personal protective equipment.

If practical changes to the process are identified which will bring about a reduction in exposure, each proposed change should be assessed on its merits (see Chapters 7 and 8) and, of course, the changes selected should be implemented. The process activities affected should then be reassessed as a check on the effectiveness of the control measure(s) in reducing the risk of damage to health.

In principle, the aim should be to control all hazards at source so that during normal operations there is no need for the use of personal protective equipment to prevent the risk of damage to health. In practice this is not always achievable, and there is often a need to protect against residual operational hazards and against unexpected and non-routine events. Having done everything reasonably practicable to control the hazards associated with an activity, the personal protection that employees will need to wear to protect against residual hazards should be identified. This should be the subject of some consultation since there is a variety of personal protective equipment available and it is important to select the right equipment for the job.

Consultation also extends to arrangements for exposure monitoring and health surveillance, which are covered in Chapters 9 and 10 respectively.

Personal protective equipment (PPE)

There are always technical considerations to make in choosing the right PPE, to ensure that whatever is chosen is capable of providing the protection necessary in a reliable way (see also p. 56). Having made this assessment, however, there is still a wide choice, and the considerations then are cost, quality and employee preference. Giving employees a choice in the PPE they will have to wear has two potential advantages:

(a) they are more likely to choose the one which is easiest for them to use and
(b) they are more likely to use the equipment because it has been their choice.

This is helpful to the employer, since the Regulations require all reasonable steps to be taken to ensure that PPE is properly used, and the more accepting employees are of the equipment they must wear, the less effort is required to ensure its proper use. Having selected the appropriate equipment, employees who are required to wear it must be instructed and trained in its use. The instruction and training must give an understanding of:

(a) why control measures are necessary
(b) what those control measures are for each hazard
(c) how and when to use the control measures and
(d) what to do in an emergency.

Information to people other than employees

Employers have a duty to provide information on hazards and control measures which affect *anyone* who carries out work (contractors, for example).

In doing so, the employer must ensure that the contractor is sufficiently knowledgeable, skilled and experienced to be able to carry out the work effectively and safely.

Summary

This chapter has dealt with employee consultation, covering the provision of information, instruction and training. It has highlighted the value of early and continuous consultation so that problem solving on hazards and exposure may be a shared process, extending into arrangements for monitoring and health surveillance.

It has also pointed out that the employer's duty to provide information about hazards and control measures extends to persons other than employees who are carrying out work on the premises.

Chapter 7
Reduction of risk by simple change

- Identify the hazardous substances
- Identify properties and hazards
- Identify the work activities
- Assess the risks
- Inform employees
- ► **Reduction of risk by simple change**
- Control the residual risks
- Check the effectiveness of control measures
- Health surveillance
- Records
- Auditing the procedures which have been put in place

Why consider process changes?

Before going directly from risk assessment into the control measures, it is worth considering whether the risks can be eliminated or reduced by making simple changes in the substances being used (by using less hazardous substances, for example) or in the activities involving those substances. If an operator is able to achieve a significant reduction in risk simply, at reasonable cost and without materially affecting the purpose or effectiveness of the process, then the effort will have been worthwhile. It may even result in a better and more cost effective process!

Looking for alternative substances and processes

Substances

Some substances may be fundamental to a process. Others, some of which may be hazardous, may not be so irreplaceable. Where a substance hazardous to health which requires additional control measures and/or personal protection is in use, consideration should be given to whether that substance could be eliminated altogether or replaced by something less hazardous or easier to control because of its physical properties.

Consider an oil/grease cleaning activity which has always used a volatile, toxic organic solvent; it may be possible to do the job adequately using a less volatile, less toxic solvent, or even to replace the organic solvent altogether with a water-based detergent.

It is sometimes possible to reduce the potential for exposure by modifying the physical form of the substance hazardous to health (eg by damping down a dusty solid before processing it). The aim should always be to use the least hazardous substance which will do the job satisfactorily.

Reducing the amount of hazardous substance being used can also reduce the need for control measures, so it is worthwhile questioning hard the need to use any more than the minimum quantity to do the job. This approach can reduce other risks, such as that of fire, from many substances hazardous to health.

The environmental effects of substances and activities should be considered before a choice is made — the substance with the least hazard to health is not always the most environmentally acceptable. Several chlorinated solvents are now controlled because of their effect on the ozone layer, and further environmental controls on solvent use are anticipated.

Activities

Changes to the activities, even very simple ones, can make a significant reduction in the potential for exposure. Using closed containers rather than open ones is one example. Allowing a product containing a volatile hazardous substance to cool before moving on to the next activity for which containment is less practical is another. Cooling reduces the vapour pressure of the hazardous substance, consequently reducing the exposure potential. Other simple examples are siphoning rather than open pouring and brushing or dipping rather than spraying. Improvements of this sort, which lead to a reduction in the release of substances hazardous to health to atmosphere, often lead to better environmental performance and less wastage.

It can be an advantage to involve employees in this stage of the hazard control process. From their close knowledge of the activity, they may readily be able to identify how the activity can be changed to reduce the exposure potential.

Where it is possible to make simple changes to reduce the potential for damage or exposure, return to the risk assessment procedure to see how this has influenced a reduction in the risk of damage.

Summary

This chapter has examined opportunities of reducing the *risk* of damage to health by reducing the *potential* for damage through elimination or substitution of the hazardous substance, and/or by reducing the potential for exposure through a reduction in quantity or alterations to the activity.

It has also indicated that such opportunities can result in cost savings, and in establishing processes which are more effective and may afford better environmental performance.

Chapter 8
Control the residual risks

- Identify the hazardous substances
- Identify properties and hazards
- Identify the work activities
- Assess the risks
- Inform employees
- Reduction of risk by simple change
- ▶ **Control the residual risks**
- Check the effectiveness of control measures
- Health surveillance
- Records
- Auditing the procedures which have been put in place

Control of exposure is regarded as adequate by the Regulations only if the exposure is reduced to as low a level as it is reasonably practicable to achieve. Where the toxic route for a substance is inhalation, it is necessary to consult the lists of occupational exposure limits (OELs) in Guidance Note EH40. If the substance in use is on the list of Maximum Exposure Limits (MELs) of the Guidance Note, the listed exposure limit should not be exceeded. Furthermore, reasonably practicable steps must be taken to reduce the airborne level below the MEL. If the substance is in the list of Occupational Exposure Standards (OESs), employers are expected to reduce exposure to at least that standard, but if exposure is exceeded the Regulations are still complied with if action is taken to reduce to the OES (or below) as soon as reasonably practicable.

If a substance is not listed in EH40, the operator will have to look further for information which can establish an Occupational Exposure Limit — for example from manufacturers or suppliers of the substance, trade associations, toxicology publications, or an occupational hygienist (see Chapter 3).

Where the toxic route for a substance is other than inhalation, EH40 has much less to offer. However, an assessment of exposure is still required. The requirement is that exposure should be controlled to a level at which "nearly all the population could be exposed repeatedly without any adverse effect". In practice, exposure by ingestion or by skin absorption is much easier to control than exposure by inhalation, and careful consideration of plant design and construction, working practices (including personal hygiene practices) and personal protective equipment should enable exposure to be reduced to nil or to a very low level.

Methods for control of exposure

Once the risk of damage to health has been reduced by making simple changes to the substances or the activities, or both, there remains the task of controlling the residual risk of damage to health. There are three steps which should be considered in order to achieve this. They are:

(a) containment (by segregation or ventilation)
(b) personal protection
(c) personal hygiene.

The Regulations are quite clear where the priorities lie in controlling exposure: "So far as is reasonably practicable, the prevention or adequate control of exposure of employees to a substance hazardous to health shall be secured by measures other than by the provision of personal protective equipment". So, personal protective equipment should always be the last resort or employed as a back-up to other methods of protection.

Any new processes should be carefully designed to minimise the potential for exposure to substances hazardous to health. In this way, the need for additional protective measures can be reduced significantly. It can be very costly to modify plant or equipment to reduce exposure after installation, compared with the cost of minimising exposure by good initial design and construction. So, when considering introducing a new process or modifying existing processes for business reasons, careful thought should be given to how exposure can be eliminated or reduced by appropriate design.

We will now examine more closely the three steps which may be used, either individually or in combination, to achieve the necessary control.

Containment (by segregation)

An obvious (although not always easy) way of reducing exposure to hazardous substances is by segregating the operator from the process. It is the same principle, operating in reverse, as that used in parts of the electronics industry, where operators are segregated from the product to protect *it* against contamination from the operators.

Segregation may be total or partial: at one extreme by completely enclosing the process and controlling it remotely, and at the other by simple screening. Physical barriers of this sort can be very effective in protecting against exposure to hazardous substances where the toxic route is skin contact or absorption.

Segregation is a good way of limiting the number of people who are exposed. For example, if operations carried out in an open-plan workplace include the use of a substance hazardous to health, including causing exposure of a number of employees to that substance, then segregating the activity from the rest of the workplace will reduce the number of people who may be exposed. Efforts can then be directed at controlling the exposure of those employees who are directly involved with the segregated activity.

The potential for exposure can be further controlled by reducing the amount of time that employees spend working close to the activity in which hazardous substances are being used, and by having a high standard of cleaning to minimise the risk of exposure from contaminated surfaces.

Containment (by ventilation)

Ventilation is the second option for containing substances hazardous to health; it is particularly appropriate where the toxic route is inhalation. Control of these substances almost inevitably involves some form of ventilation, but it is still well worthwhile considering containment by segregation first, since ventilation can be expensive, particularly if it is being applied to large work areas which have to be heated.

Ventilation solutions can range from the very simple to the very complex. Both natural and forced ventilation may be considered. The precise nature of the ventilation will be dependent on the risk of damage to health derived from the assessment of the damage potential of the substance, on the exposure potential of the activity, and knowledge of where the lack of containment is occurring. A common method of containing localised exposure from an activity is to identify where the lack of containment is occurring, partially segregate that area by means of an enclosure and apply local exhaust ventilation (LEV) to the enclosure.

Having introduced containment measures, it is essential that they are used adequately by employees. This is a responsibility both of the employer and the employee. The employer must instruct and train employees in the use of the containment measures, keeping a check that employees are using those containment measures properly and taking remedial action where necessary. Employees must use the containment measures in compliance with the instruction and training received (see Chapter 6 for detail).

Personal protection

As we have already established, personal protection is the last resort for the control of exposure of employees to substances hazardous to health. Provision should be made for routine work, for foreseeable deviations from routine and for emergencies. Examples of situations where the use of suitable personal protective equipment may be necessary include the following:

(a) where adequate control of exposure cannot be achieved by process or engineering controls alone
(b) in emergency situations, where personal protective equipment is necessary to protect operators whilst the situation is brought under control
(c) where an assessment indicates that further measures

are necessary to protect against exposure, until those further measures have been introduced and proved effective

(d) during maintenance operations, where it is perceived that there may be a risk of exposure.

There is an extremely wide range of PPE available such as eye, hand and respiratory protection. Most importantly, the equipment must match the needs of the protection required from the potential exposure.

The Personal Protective Equipment at Work Regulations 1992 (and their accompanying guidance) give comprehensive information on the provision, selection, maintenance, use of and training in PPE.

Where there is a design and production standard for PPE (for example a British Standard), the equipment which meets that standard should always be chosen. Choice of a particular type of PPE should be made, taking into account its ability to resist penetration by the substance(s), and how it will affect the movement, mobility, vision, etc of the user. Respiratory protective equipment must be selected with great care to ensure it is of a standard which is approved by the Health and Safety Executive (HSE), and is suitable for the purpose. Lists of approved respiratory protective equipment are published by the HSE. Where more than one item of PPE needs to be worn, the combined effect on the wearer should be considered.

As with containment measures, both employers and employees have a responsibility to ensure that the personal protective equipment is used adequately.

The employer must instruct and train employees in the use of personal protective equipment, must ensure that the equipment is adequately maintained (where this is necessary to make certain that it remains effective and suitable for use) and must check that employees are using the equipment adequately, taking remedial action where necessary. Employees must also be instructed in the removal and disposal of contaminated PPE, and the employer must make adequate provision for the cleaning (where appropriate) and disposal of contaminated equipment.

Employees are responsible for using the equipment according to the instruction and training they have received, and for reporting any faults in anything provided to protect against exposure to hazardous substances, whether these are containment measures or personal protective equipment.

Personal hygiene

The final step is control of personal hygiene. Decisions may have to be made about restriction or exclusion of eating, drinking and smoking in the workplace, depending on the risk and consequences of exposure to substances hazardous to health from workplace activities. Where such hygiene restrictions are necessary, they should be closely enforced, and suitable provision made for employees to eat, drink and smoke whilst at work. This provision should include changing (where necessary) and washing facilities located so that they are convenient, and designed in such a way that cross-contamination is avoided.

Particular care is needed in the arrangements for the removal of PPE which may be contaminated. This should take into account the potential for exposure to fumes or dust from contaminated clothing during removal, and storage of contaminated equipment to avoid cross-contamination of employees or their clothing. Careful segregation of clean and contaminated (or potentially contaminated) PPE is needed.

Again, the responsibility for ensuring that suitable hygiene measures are taken rests both with the employer and the employee. The employer is responsible for providing suitable hygiene procedures and facilities, and the employees are responsible for using those procedures and facilities in accordance with the instruction and training they have been given.

Special arrangements for handling carcinogens

The COSHH (Amendment) Regulations 1992 demand special arrangements to control exposure to a carcinogen where exposure cannot be prevented by using an alternative substance or process. The special arrangements are detailed in a schedule to the Regulations.

Summary

This chapter has explored ways of controlling risks of damage to health, from the preferred option of containment by segregation and/or ventilation to personal protection and personal hygiene. The use of PPE as a last line of defence, rather than as a primary means of control, has been re-emphasised.

Whatever means of control are employed, they must be carefully chosen, maintained and properly used; both employers and employees have a duty to ensure that this happens.

Chapter 9

Check the effectiveness of control measures

- Identify the hazardous substances
- Identify properties and hazards
- Identify the work activities
- Assess the risks
- Inform employees
- Reduction of risk by simple change
- Control the residual risks
- ▸ **Check the effectiveness of control measures**
- Health surveillance
- Records
- Auditing the procedures which have been put in place

When the risks have been assessed and the measures to eliminate or control exposure have been identified and put in place, those control measures must be maintained. Checks may also be needed to make sure that the control measures are satisfactory, both initially and on an ongoing basis. It is not always evident that the control measures are working effectively, especially where airborne substances hazardous to health are involved.

There are four steps that can be taken to support and check on control measures:

(a) checks on engineering controls
(b) checks on personal protective equipment (especially respiratory protective equipment)
(c) exposure monitoring
(d) health surveillance.

The first of these concerns the maintenance of the controls designed to contain exposure (eg ventilation systems). The second concerns the maintenance of equipment used as the final line of defence against exposure to hazardous substances. The third is the measurement of the amount of substances hazardous to health to which the employee is exposed despite the control measures. The fourth is a check to identify any adverse health effects from the use of substances hazardous to health in the workplace.

Checks are always required on engineering controls and personal protective equipment: the need for exposure monitoring and health surveillance depends on the substances used and the conditions of their use.

Let us take each of the four items in turn.

Checks on engineering controls

The basic requirement of COSHH is that where control measures are provided to ensure the prevention or adequate control of exposure, they should be maintained in efficient working order and in good repair.

What general checks are necessary?

The General Approved Code of Practice to the COSHH Regulations deals with the maintenance, examination and testing of control measures at length. Where possible, engineering controls should be visually inspected at least once a week. This can usually be done relatively easily, for example by checking whether extraction fan pulley belts are slipping, that motors are running smoothly, that ventilation trunking is not displaced or damaged, that filters and collectors (for dust extract systems) are not choked or full and that exhaust outlets are not blocked. A rough indication that extract ventilation is functioning at the point of extraction can be made by permanently installed flutter tapes or by periodic use of simple "smoke tubes". Any visible or audible signs that engineering controls are not functioning as normal should be followed up as soon as possible.

A system of preventive maintenance by a competent person should be established for all engineering controls, specifying the items that need servicing, the nature of the work, the service schedule and the requirements for repair or replacement.

In general, how often should checks be made?

The frequency of checking for individual engineering controls depends on the reliability of each of them and the consequences of their failure or deterioration on the exposure of employees to substances hazardous to health. If the engineering control is prone to rapid deterioration or frequent failure, or if its effective operation is critical to preventing exposure which could lead to a serious risk of damage to health, then maintenance checks should be sufficiently frequent to counteract that risk of failure or significant deterioration.

As equipment ages, the frequency of inspection may need to be increased, since increasing age is often accompanied by an increased rate of deterioration or failure. Where significant changes are made to the engineering controls, a reassessment should be made of the effectiveness of the controls against the original risk assessment (see Chapter 5) and of the need for any new testing and examination requirements.

Requirements for local exhaust ventilation (LEV)

LEV should be thoroughly examined and tested at least once every 14 months, to include the following information:

(a) the name and location of the equipment, and the date of its last thorough maintenance check
(b) the conditions of operation at the time of the test
(c) the performance criteria for the equipment (ie what measurable standard should it achieve to demonstrate it is operating to its required performance)
(d) its measured performance in relation to the performance criteria
(e) corrective action to be taken if measured performance is worse than the performance criteria
(f) the signature of the person carrying out the maintenance check
(g) where corrective action has to be taken, the details of the repairs carried out and the results of the test following the repair work.

Performance criteria can include air flow in a ducting, extract face velocity or static pressure across a filter. Whatever criterion is chosen, it must be a real indicator of the ability of the engineering control to satisfy the requirements of the original risk assessment.

Special requirements

In certain specific cases, more frequent testing and examination of LEV is required. These cases, such as those involving blasting and grinding of metals and other fume producing processes relating to metal casting, are detailed in schedule 3 of the Regulations.

Checks on personal protective equipment (PPE)

All PPE will deteriorate with use, gradually reducing its protection. The frequency of checks on, and changing of, PPE will depend on the nature of the substance for which the personal protection is being used, and the type of personal protection itself. There are two basic types of protection:

(a) protection against skin (including eye) contact
(b) protection against inhalation.

Skin contact

There is a variety of personal protection for eyes and skin, from goggles to full protective suits. The materials are usually rubber or plastic, and periodic visual checks are needed to detect breaks in the material or stiffening and cracking which indicate that the material is deteriorating. Where this is detected the protective equipment should be discarded and replaced.

PPE should be kept as free as possible from contamination by the substance hazardous to health, especially where it is known that the PPE has limited resistance to penetration by the substance. For example, many chlorinated solvents will penetrate most protective rubber gloves after a relatively short period of time, so operations in which protective gloves are constantly exposed to the solvent, or heavy solvent vapour, should be avoided.

Inhalation (respiratory protective equipment)

Careful maintenance of respiratory protective equipment (RPE) is essential, since it is not always easy to check visually if it is performing efficiently. Other than disposable respiratory equipment (eg disposable dust masks), the COSHH Approved Code of Practice requires thorough examination, and testing where appropriate, of RPE at least once a month. If conditions of use are particularly severe, the frequency of examination and testing should be increased; if used infrequently with airborne substances of relatively low toxicity, examination and testing may be less frequent. So, a monthly test is a good baseline, with the actual frequency depending on the conditions of use and the respiratory protection itself; the decision on the required frequency should be taken by a competent person.

Examination of RPE should include a thorough visual examination by a competent person of all the parts which may deteriorate with time, from retaining straps to filters and valves, motors supplying clean air and air compression systems. Where RPE is air fed the flow and quality of the air supply should be tested. A list of "approved" RPE is published by the Health and Safety Executive and maintenance requirements for various types of equipment are detailed in the British Standards. If any defects are found by the examination and test, they should be made good before the equipment is used again.

Records of examination and testing of RPE are detailed in Chapter 11.

Exposure monitoring

What is exposure monitoring?

Exposure monitoring is simply the testing and measuring of the actual exposure of a person to a substance hazardous to health, as a check that the containment measures are effective in eliminating exposure or reducing it to an acceptable level.

Monitoring varies from very simple techniques, such as using indicator paper to detect the presence of acid vapour or mist, to relatively complex techniques requiring skilled sampling and analysis (eg the measurement of airborne asbestos).

When is monitoring necessary?

Monitoring should be carried out:

(a) where it is necessary to check on the effectiveness of control measures
(b) where it is necessary to confirm that MELs or OESs, or any other established standards are not exceeded
(c) where failure in control measures could result in serious damage to health.

The need for monitoring mainly depends on the reliability of the control measures. It is usually appropriate to check the effectiveness of newly established control measures, unless they are such that containment is without doubt. Monitoring is mandatory for a small number of operations, such as where vinyl chloride monomer is being used and for chromium plating processes.

What are the procedures for monitoring?

Planning for monitoring should take into account *where* sampling of the atmosphere should be taken, *when* it should be taken, *what* method of sampling should be used, *what analysis technique* is appropriate for measuring the amount of substance sampled and *how to interpret* the results. Again, all this should be carried out by a competent person.

Always use the simplest reliable technique available and carry out sampling in the places where, and at times when, exposure is most likely to occur. If the detection and analysis of the substances is difficult or complex, an option is to substitute, for the purposes of monitoring, the hazardous substance with another substance which has similar physical characteristics, but which is easier to detect and analyse (and, if possible, less toxic!). EH42 is a useful Health and Safety

Executive Guidance Note, available from HMSO, which details general methods of monitoring and analysis. Sampling and analysis techniques for specific substances are contained in the MDHS (Methods for the Determination of Hazardous Substances) series produced by the Health and Safety Executive. The series now comprises over 60 techniques and is constantly being extended.

The requirements for keeping records of monitoring are described in Chapter 11.

When is health surveillance necessary?

The Regulations require health surveillance of employees working with any of the substances used in the processes described in schedule 5 of the Regulations, unless exposure is insignificant. These are certain established carcinogens. There is also a requirement to carry out health surveillance where exposure to a substance hazardous to health is likely to cause an identifiable disease or adverse health effect, and where there are valid techniques for detecting the effect. Examples of this are substances which are known to cause occupational asthma or severe dermatitis, or which are of recognised systemic toxicity.

If the services of a Medical Officer are not available, advice about the need for health surveillance may be obtained from HSE's local employment medical adviser. Where surveillance is considered to be necessary, it should be carried out under the direction of an employment medical adviser or other qualified doctor at intervals not less than 12 months.

The requirements for keeping records are discussed in Chapter 11.

Facilities for health surveillance

Where health surveillance is carried out at the employer's place of work, suitable facilities must be provided to carry out the surveillance in adequate conditions of privacy, comfort and hygiene.

Health surveillance is covered in detail in Chapter 10.

Summary

In this chapter we have explored in some detail the checks necessary to maintain the effectiveness both of the control measures and of PPE by scheduled examination, testing and maintenance. We have also examined the requirements for checks by atmospheric monitoring on the effectiveness of the control measures and referred to the requirements for health monitoring to detect, at an early stage, any adverse health effects of employees. Effective planning and implementation of these checks is vital in order to obtain results upon which appropriate action can be taken to maintain the effectiveness of control measures.

Chapter 10
Health surveillance

- Identify the hazardous substances
- Identify properties and hazards
- Identify the work activities
- Assess the risks
- Inform employees
- Reduction of risk by simple change
- Control the residual risks
- Check the effectiveness of control measures
- ▸ **Health surveillance**
- Records
- Auditing the procedures which have been put in place

Why health surveillance?

The overriding requirement of the COSHH Regulations is that any personal exposure to substances hazardous to health should be either eliminated or minimised below the point at which those substances may cause ill health. Because of the nature of some substances and processes, however, it is not always possible to be absolutely sure that there is no personal exposure, despite containment control measures and PPE. It is in these circumstances that health surveillance may be necessary. The primary aims of health surveillance are to detect any adverse health effects due to exposure to substances hazardous to health as early as possible so that action can be taken to remove the person from the source of the exposure and to review the effectiveness of measures taken to control the danger.

We have already seen that health surveillance of employees is the final step in the sequence of measures designed to protect against substances hazardous to health. Control measures taken to protect employees should be based on the best available information on the properties of the substances and their effect on the body. For some substances this effect is well known, and the associated disease or adverse medical condition is also well known and readily detected. In these situations health surveillance can play a positive role in checking the effectiveness of containment measures and PPE in controlling exposure.

The effects of many substances on the body are not fully understood and the associated medical conditions not so specific or well-characterised. In these situations it is not easy to identify specific health abnormalities related to exposure, although keeping general health records can detect health trends which may give an early indication of excessive exposure.

Exposure to substances affects different people to varying degrees. Some people react adversely to levels of exposure at which others suffer no apparent ill effect — in some cases this can occur well below the Occupational Exposure Limit. Some allergic reactions are common examples of this higher than normal sensitivity to exposure. Additionally, some substances, particularly those which are recognised sensitisers, may affect individuals at extremely low levels, following sensitisation from previous exposure.

The level of damage which may be caused to an individual by exposure to substances hazardous to health is, therefore, a combination of the harmful properties of the substance itself, the amount of the substance to which the individual is exposed, the length of exposure, the route of exposure and the sensitivity of the individual to the substance. Where there is exposure to more than one substance, an additional complication can be synergistic adverse effect — that is, one substance greatly increases the adverse health effect caused by another. An example is smoking and exposure to asbestos dust.

In summary, the effect of exposure to substances hazardous to health can be complex and health surveillance has an important part to play in checking the effectiveness of measures taken to eliminate or minimise exposure, by detecting any adverse health effects as early as possible.

When is health surveillance necessary?

The "decision tree" in Figure 15 is designed to help answer this question. Firstly, employers using any of the substances listed in schedule 5 of the Regulations must arrange for health surveillance of employees who may be exposed to the scheduled substances, although if exposure is assessed as insignificant, health surveillance will not be required. But, a careful check must be kept on the effectiveness of the measures used to keep that exposure insignificant, in order to demonstrate that health surveillance continues to be unnecessary.

The next check is whether substances which are known to cause adverse health effects are being used. There is no definitive list of substances to which exposure may cause occupational disease or ill health, although the list of "prescribed industrial diseases" issued by the Department of Social Security is a good start. By inference, exposure to any substance for which there is an Occupational Exposure Limit (HSE Guidance Note EH40) may cause ill health. As a guide, if the substances being used are hazardous to health and it is not possible to confirm that exposure of employees (or anyone else who may be affected by the operation) is insignificant (at least below the Occupational Exposure Limit) then health surveillance should seriously be considered. The more hazardous the substance, the lower the level of exposure at which adverse health effect is likely, and the stronger the case for health surveillance. The COSHH General Approved Code of Practice describes some categories of substance that will usually require health surveillance, although the list is by no means definitive. Much more practical guidance is available from the HSE booklet *Health Surveillance Under COSHH: Guidance for Employers* (HMSO), from the Chemical Industries Association booklet *Guidance on Health Surveillance*, and from the HSE booklet *Surveillance of People Exposed to Health Risks at Work*.

For some substances (notably human carcinogens, respiratory sensitisers and biologically active agents) there is no safe level of exposure and in these circumstances health surveillance will almost always be needed.

The greater the reliance on PPE to prevent exposure to substances hazardous to health, the stronger the case for health surveillance, since it can be difficult to maintain control over the effective use of PPE.

What does health surveillance involve?

The extent and type of health surveillance depends mainly on the nature of the ill health effect which is known to accompany exposure. In its broadest form, however, it comprises health surveys, examination, inspection and testing of individuals at appropriate intervals by a suitably qualified person, recording of the results and maintenance and review of individual health records.

An additional feature of health surveillance is the review of general trends in the health of the population of employees having potential exposure, compared with those with no exposure. Note, however, that *health* surveillance does not always mean surveillance by a medical practitioner.

In some cases, a simple health record is all that is required. This comprises basic personal details and a historical record of jobs involving exposure to substances requiring health surveillance. The HSE booklet *Health Surveillance Under COSHH: Guidance for Employers* gives examples of those circumstances in which health records only need to be kept.

In other cases, medical monitoring may be necessary. For example, if exposure to a substance hazardous to health results in visible signs of ill health, then simple, regular visual inspection will be appropriate. Some substances hazardous to health are metabolised in, and excreted by, the body as readily detectable substances. For example, exposure to benzene will result in the excretion of phenol in the urine. Exposure to substances which affect the respiratory system (isocyanates, for example) may produce detectable changes in lung function, which again can be measured.

There are many different ways of measuring the effects of exposure to substances hazardous to health, but a decision has to be made on the type of health surveillance required. For substances listed in schedule 5 of the Regulations where the risk of exposure to the substance has been assessed as significant, health surveillance under the supervision of an employment medical adviser (HSE employed medical practitioners experienced in occupational health) or appointed doctor (appointed in writing by the HSE) is

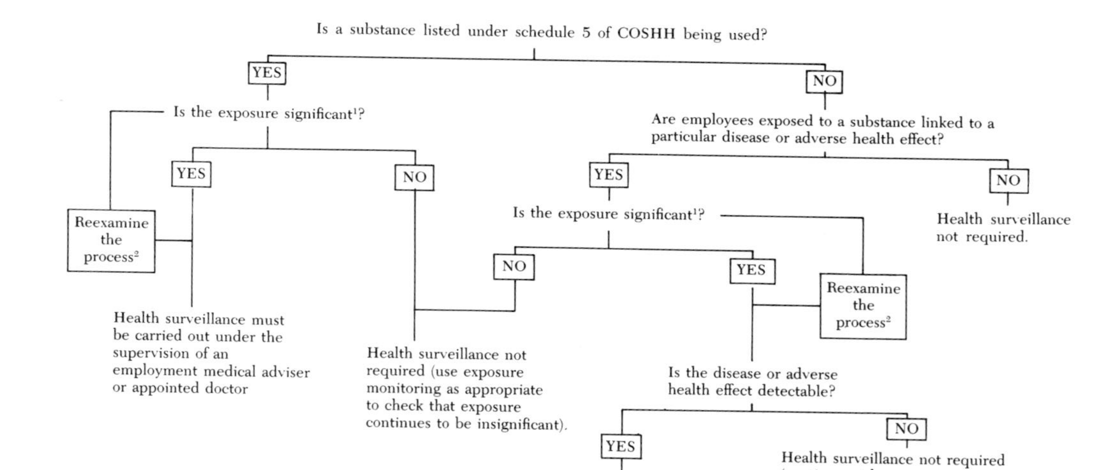

1. Is there a reasonable likelihood that the disease or adverse health effect will occur under the conditions of exposure?
2. Examine ways of reducing exposure by process modification or use of engineering controls.

Figure 15 Health surveillance guide

mandatory. These advisers will specify the health surveillance required and will be involved in the monitoring programme.

For all other circumstances where health surveillance is required, the employer has to make the decision about the appropriate level of surveillance. If the employer already makes use of a doctor with training in occupational medicine, that doctor will probably be involved in general health monitoring and in assessing health surveillance requirements. If not, the employer should seek advice about the form of health surveillance required from a doctor with occupational health training (a qualification from the Faculty of Occupational Medicine, for example). Alternatively, employers can seek advice from the nearest Employment Medical Advisory Service (EMAS), which may either help directly or identify a suitable occupational health adviser.

Having decided whether health surveillance is required, and what form this should take, the employer has to decide who should carry it out, and how often. Again, this will depend on whether a simple health record is sufficient or whether some form of additional medical monitoring is required. The occupational health adviser should be able to advise on the appropriate people to carry out health surveillance. This may range from

(a) the employees themselves (self-examination and reporting to a nominated responsible person)
(b) suitably trained supervisors
(c) occupational first aiders
(d) an occupational nurse
(e) a doctor.

The choice will depend on the level of skill and training required for the type of health surveillance needed.

Decisions on the frequency of monitoring will normally be made as part of the overall assessment of health surveillance needs. In some cases (for example substances listed in schedule 5 of the Regulations) this will be predetermined; in many others there will be some broad guidelines based on experience and established good practice. Again, an occupational health adviser will be able to judge the frequency of surveillance required.

In some cases, particularly where the disease or ill health

associated with exposure to a substance hazardous to health has a long period of latency, health surveillance has to be continued even after exposure has ceased. An example is health surveillance of employees working with human carcinogens, in order than any initial onset of cancer can be detected and treated in its very early stages.

Records

Keeping records is an essential part of health surveillance. The necessary records are described in the Appendix to the General Approved Code of Practice. Suitable forms are provided in Croner's *Record Keeping Book for COSHH*. The minimum requirement is the collection, maintenance and review of health records. Some examples of substances for which health records only are required are given in the General Approved Code of Practice.

If medical monitoring is carried out, records of the results of the monitoring will be required in addition to the general health record. All records of health surveillance must be kept in a suitable form and should be easily referenced to other relevant monitoring records. Health surveillance records must be kept for at least 40 years from the date of the last entry, and must be made available at all times for inspection by an employment medical adviser or appointed doctor, when required by the HSE.

Involvement of employees

For health surveillance to be effective, the full understanding and co-operation of employees is important. They need to understand why the health surveillance is being carried out, what it will entail for them and what they themselves are required to do. This may be as simple as an annual review of their general health or it may involve periodic examination or medical checking. In some cases it will be important for employees to self-monitor for signs of disease or ill health and to report any such indications to a responsible person nominated by the employer. Whatever the health surveillance requirements, adequate facilities should be provided to enable health surveillance, in whatever form it takes, to be carried out in conditions of adequate hygiene, comfort and privacy.

Evidence of adverse health effect

Any signs or symptoms which indicate ill health or disease require prompt attention. All suspected cases of ill health should be referred to a qualified medical practitioner, preferably to a doctor with further qualifications in occupational medicine.

Additionally, the employer will have to decide if the case is reportable to the HSE under the Reporting of Injuries, Diseases and Dangerous Occurrences Regulations 1985 (RIDDOR).

In such circumstances, the arrangements for controlliing exposure will need to be reviewed to identify how the exposure leading to ill health has occurred. This should indicate shortcomings in the original COSHH assessment, or failures in the containment measures or the personal protective equipment used to control exposure, indicating what needs to be done to bring exposure under control.

Chapter 11
Records

- Identify the hazardous substances
- Identify properties and hazards
- Identify the work activities
- Assess the risks
- Inform employees
- Reduction of risk by simple change
- Control the residual risks
- Check the effectiveness of control measures
- Health surveillance
- ▸ **Records**
- Auditing the procedures which have been put in place

One of the requirements of COSHH is that the employer should be able to demonstrate compliance. This can only be achieved in practice by keeping records of assessments, maintenance, monitoring and the other activities needed to check, or to confirm, compliance. The Regulations are quite specific about when records are required. Records are the only effective means of preserving how, for example, decisions on risk assessment were made, so that the decision making can be reproduced in future assessments.

Activities for which records should be made, and kept (where relevant) are:

(a) risk assessments
(b) maintenance of control measures, including
  (i) engineering controls
  (ii) respiratory protective equipment (RPE)
(c) monitoring
(d) health surveillance.

Other records, not specifically required by COSHH, may be necessary: employee training is a notable example.

As an aid to effective record keeping a *Record Keeping Book* (containing suitable forms) is available from Croner Publications.

Risk assessments

Except in the simplest and most obvious cases which can be easily repeated and explained at any time, risk assessments should be recorded. There are many ways of doing this and the forms in *Croner's Record Keeping Book for COSHH* include general assessments and the assessment of emergency provisions.

The risk assessment record should be retained as long as the activity (or activities) to which it relates does not change. The regulations do not indicate how long a risk assessment should be kept when it is replaced or revised. However, it is worthwhile considering keeping assessments for a reasonable period of time in case any retrospective questioning of potential exposure arises.

Maintenance of control measures

Engineering controls

In Chapter 9 we examined the requirements for the frequency of examination and testing of engineering controls. The Regulations are quite specific about the records needed for examination and testing of local exhaust ventilation, which are detailed in the *Record Keeping Book for COSHH*. For all engineering controls, similar information should be recorded which is appropriate to the engineering control being tested.

To illustrate how detailed COSHH is with regard to the maintenance of control measures, for equipment, a record of the following information should be kept:

(a) specific identification of the equipment
(b) the hazardous substance(s) for which the equipment is being used
(c) date of the previous examination and test

(d) operating conditions at the time of test (abnormal operating conditions should be recorded)
(e) the required performance standard of the equipment, and the test methods used to judge its performance
(f) performance on the test (to compare against the required performance)
(g) action taken (if the equipment did not meet the required performance)
(h) date of the examination and test
(i) identification of the employer of the person carrying out the examination
(j) signature of the person carrying out the examination
(k) details of any modification, adjustment or repair carried out.

Where action is required to improve the effectiveness of the local exhaust ventilation (LEV) to bring it up to the required performance standard, a second examination and test should be carried out to confirm it is operating to specification.

It is important to have a performance standard for all LEV against which to judge its operating effectiveness. This performance standard may be an indirect measurement (such as pressure drop across a filter) or a more direct measurement (for example, flow in the ducting or face velocity at an opening). Whatever the performance standard, it should relate directly to the required effectiveness of containment. It is particularly important to bear this in mind when making even minor changes to the process or activity which may make the performance standard invalid for measuring containment capability. Records of the tests (or at least a suitable summary) on LEV should be kept for at least five years from the date of the test. COSHH also specifies record keeping requirements for respiratory protective equipment in particular, and personal protection equipment in general.

Respiratory protective equipment (RPE)

The requirements for examination and testing of RPE were explored in Chapter 9, and the requirements for recording those checks are equally specific. Any RPE, other than one-shift disposable respirators, should be subject to regular checks, which are described in Chapter 9. Records of these checks should include the following information:

(a) name and address of the employer responsible for the RPE
(b) sufficient details of the equipment in order to identify it individually
(c) date of the check and the name and signature of the checker
(d) condition of the equipment and any defects found
(e) the pressure of air or oxygen in the supply cylinder, where appropriate
(f) the volume, flow and quality of the air (for airline fed equipment).

Monitoring

Whatever format is used to keep monitoring records, it should at least include the following information:

(a) where the monitoring was done
(b) the time and duration of the monitoring
(c) the monitoring method(s) used
(d) the operating conditions under which the monitoring was carried out
(e) if personal sampling was carried out, the names of the individuals concerned
(f) the results of the monitoring.

If the results of the monitoring indicate that the level of contaminant in the atmosphere is greater than the exposure standard, both the action taken to reduce that level and the subsequent monitoring to confirm that the exposure standard has been met as a result of the action taken should be recorded.

Again, records of monitoring must be kept for at least five years. Where the record relates to the exposure of identifiable individuals, however, they must be kept for at least 40 years.

Where health records are also kept, the monitoring records should be maintained in a way that enables easy comparison between the two.

Health surveillance records

Where health surveillance is required by the Regulations, the health records should contain at least the information required by the COSHH Approved Code of Practice. Records of health surveillance should be kept in a way that enables easy comparison with any monitoring records.

Records of health surveillance which is carried out to monitor the health of employees who are, or may be, exposed to substances hazardous to health, must be kept for at least 30 years from the date of the last entry.

Training

Although the Regulations do not require the employer to keep records of training of employees, they do require the employer to take "all reasonable steps" to ensure that any control measure, or personal protective equipment, provided to prevent or control exposure to hazardous substances is properly used. Because this involves training of employees in the proper use of control measures and personal protective equipment, it is advisable to keep training records to be able to demonstrate that the requirement to take "all reasonable steps" has been met.

Some training will need to be repeated periodically, or renewed if control measures or personal protective equipment change, so it is an advantage to use records as a prompt for recall for refresher training.

Summary

This chapter has outlined the types of records which should be kept to demonstrate compliance with the Regulations. Records may be in any form, provided that the essential details are kept, and provided that they are held in a form which is easy to understand and, in the case of monitoring and health surveillance records, which enables easy comparison between the two. Records must be made available to inspectors of relevant enforcing authorities (such as the Health and Safety Executive), and some records (eg assessments and monitoring records) should be made available to employees or their representatives on request.

Chapter 12

Auditing the procedures which have been put in place

- Identify the hazardous substances
- Identify properties and hazards
- Identify the work activities
- Assess the risks
- Inform employees
- Reduction of risk by simple change
- Control the residual risks
- Check the effectiveness of control measures
- Health surveillance
- Records
- ► **Auditing the procedures which have been put in place**

Carrying out COSHH assessments, defining maintenance, testing and examination schedules for control measures, identifying any necessary PPE, informing and instructing employees, establishing monitoring and, where necessary, setting up health surveillance, all backed up by a suitable recording system, go to make up compliance with the COSHH Regulations. In addition, formal operating procedures in support of these arrangements will serve to *maintain* that compliance.

It is a fact, however, that all systems and procedures gradually lose their effectiveness or become outdated unless they are adequately audited. No-one, for example, would continue to run a business without having a periodic audit as a check on the financial health of the business. In just the same way, COSHH control procedures should be audited to ensure they remain effective.

Remember what is required to satisfy the Regulations:

(a) risk assessments
(b) control measures (including PPE)
(c) monitoring
(d) records and
(e) employee compliance.

All these elements should be audited to check that what is in place to ensure compliance is still effective. To measure this compliance requires a yardstick — an audit standard. For example, the audit standard for a COSHH risk assessment may be that:

(a) there is an up-to-date assessment, with an assessment record number
(b) all the substances hazardous to health have been identified
(c) all the relevant parts of the risk assessment form have been filled in
(d) the critical control measures have been identified
(e) personal protective equipment, monitoring and health surveillance requirements (where appropriate) are identified
(f) a nominated competent person has signed the assessment.

There are others, depending on the situation. Having set the audit standard, each of the assessments can be audited against it. The same principle can be applied to control measures, personal protective equipment, monitoring, records and employee compliance.

For employee compliance, for example, it is helpful to apply the following audit standard:

(a) the employee understands and follows operating procedures where they relate to prevention or control of exposure to substances hazardous to health
(b) the employee understands the role and operation of control measures designed to prevent or control

exposure to substances hazardous to health, and operates those control measures effectively

(c) the employee understands how, when and where to use PPE, and is seen to do so

(d) the employee understands, and follows, the hygiene measures necessary to prevent or control exposure to substances hazardous to health

and so on.

These steps mean that employee compliance is measured in a comprehensive and systematic way each time, and in a way which records the outcome and identifies areas of weakness, or non-conformance, upon which action can be taken.

It is usually a good idea to audit comprehensively at least annually. That will be frequent enough for the less critical items, but for the more crucial ones, more frequent auditing may be necessary. An example would be where the effective operation of a control measure, or the effective use or maintenance of personal protective equipment, is crucial in the control of a substance hazardous to health. In this case, auditing the effectiveness of the control, or employee compliance in using the equipment, would need to be more frequent than annually.

Finally, be wary of changes, however insignificant they appear to be. Even small changes in a control measure, in a substance, in an activity in which a substance is used, or in PPE, can substantially affect the control of exposure. Treat any changes in activities, substances, control measures, etc as modifications to COSHH controls—modifications which require a formal, and recordable, reappraisal of the original COSHH assessment. Often, this will be a simple formality, but having a modification procedure in place will ensure that small, but significant, changes do not go by unchecked. And, having established this modification procedure, it will need to be audited, like everything else required by COSHH: the COSHH (Amendment) Regulations 1992 require assessments to be made on a regular basis regardless of the level of risk of exposure or the nature of the substances to which people may be exposed.

Summary

This chapter rounds off by making the point that COSHH assessments are not a "one off" process. Whenever substances, activities, engineering controls or personal protective equipment are changed, then check to see how this affects the original assessment. Finally, periodically audit activities to make sure that the provisions for the protection of employees and others made as a result of assessments are working, and to pick up any significant, unassessed changes since the last assessment.

In this way, an employer can be confident that he or she will continue to meet the requirements of the COSHH Regulations — the protection of individuals from substances hazardous to health — and that early efforts in carrying out assessments and establishing controls have not been wasted.

Appendix
Bibliography

1. The Control of Substances Hazardous to Health Regulations, 1988 (SI 1988 No. 1657, HMSO).
2. The Control of Substances Hazardous to Health (Amendment) Regulations 1991 (SI 1991 No. 2431, HMSO).
3. The Control of Substances Hazardous to Health (Amendment) Regulations 1992 (SI 1992 No. 2382, HMSO).
4. L5 The Control of Substances Hazardous to Health General Approved Code of Practice and Control of Carcinogenic Substances Approved Code of Practice (HMSO, 4th edn., ISBN 0 11 882085 0).
5. Approved Code of Practice COP 30 Control of Substances Hazardous to Health in Fumigation Operations (HMSO, ISBN 0 11 885469 0).
6. Approved Code of Practice COP 31 Control of Vinyl Chloride at Work (HMSO, ISBN 0 11 885934 X).
7. Approved Code of Practice COP 41 Control of Substances Hazardous to Health in the Production of Pottery (HMSO, ISBN 0 11 885530 1).
8. Approved Code of Practice L9 The Safe Use of Pesticides for Non-Agricultural Purposes (HMSO, ISBN 0 11 885673 1).
9. The Classification Packaging and Labelling of Dangerous Substances Regulations 1984 (SI 1984 No. 1244, amended by 1986/1922, 1988/766, 1989/2208 and 1990/1255).
10. The Personal Protective Equipment at Work Regulations 1992 (SI 1992 No. 2966, HMSO).
11. L25 Personal Protective Equipment at Work: Guidance on Regulations (HMSO, ISBN 0 11 886334 7).
12. Respiratory Protective Equipment: Legislative

Requirements and Lists of HSE Approved Standards and Type Approved Equipment (HMSO, ISBN 0 11 886382 7).
13. HSE Guidance Booklet HS(G)97 A Step-by-Step Guide to COSHH Assessments (HMSO, ISBN 0 11 886379 7).
14. HSE Guidance Note EH40: Occupational Exposure Limits (HMSO, revised annually).
15. HSE Guidance Note EH42: Monitoring Strategies for Toxic Substances (HMSO, ISBN 0 11 885412 7).
16. Control of Substances Hazardous to Health in the Construction Industry (HMSO, ISBN 0 11 885432 1).
17. Health Surveillance under COSHH (HMSO, ISBN 0 11 885447 X).
18. COSHH: Guidance for Universities, Polytechnics and Colleges of Further Education (HMSO, ISBN 0 11 885433 X).
19. The Application of COSHH to Plastics Processing (HMSO, ISBN 0 11 885556 5).
20. The Control of Substances Hazardous to Health: Guidance for the Initial Assessment in Hospitals (HMSO ISBN 0 11 321262 3).
21. Dare, P R M, Record Keeping Book for COSHH (Croner Publications Ltd, updated annually).
22. Substances Hazardous to Health (Croner Publications Ltd, updated quarterly).
23. Kellard, B, Hazardous Substances: Carcinogens Guide (Croner Publications Ltd, 2nd edn., ISBN 1 85524 227 3).
24. Houston, A (ed.), Dangerous Chemicals: Emergency First Aid Guide (Croner Publications Ltd, ISBN 0 900319 43 7).
25. Warren, P J (ed.), Dangerous Chemicals: Emergency Spillage Guide (Croner Publications Ltd, 2nd edn., ISBN 0 900319 39 9).
26. Surveillance of People Exposed to Health Risks at Work (HMSO, ISBN 0 11 885574 3).

Index